LITTLEMORE

Portrait by Maria Giberne
of John Henry Newman as a young man

LITTLEMORE

An Oxfordshire
Village, Then and Now

by

George F. Tull

The King's England Press

2002

ISBN 1 872438 42 3

Littlemore: An Oxfordshire Village, Then and Now
is typeset by Moose Manuscripts
in Times New Roman and published by
The King's England Press Ltd,
Cambertown House, Commercial Road, Goldthorpe,
Rotherham, South Yorkshire, S63 9BL.

Printed and bound in Great Britain by

Woolnough Bookbinding
Irthlingborough
Northamptonshire

Author's Note

I well remember in my grandmother's lifetime hearing from her of a travelling author, by the name of William J. Monk, who used to sell his own booklets about Oxfordshire. I have two of them and find them delightfully informative and well produced. As far as I know, Mr. Monk never wrote of Littlemore. That could have provided me with an incentive to fill in the gap, but there were stronger motives, historical rather than topographical. The result is what follows. I hope it may stimulate wider interest in the subject.

G.F.T.

Memories live in trees and walls,
in places undisturbed
and not at first apparent;

Memories from time before our time,
of those we have not seen,
who kept their seasonal ways;

And here, across the lapse of time,
heart speaks to heart
with never need of words –
COR AD COR LOQUITUR

Introduction

"Often it seems one needs to turn aside from the thundrous highways to search out the real England, the quiet retreat of our national spirit."

> \- Anon.

"I do not ask to see
The distant scene -"

> \- J. H. Newman.

To begin our exploration in a practical way, a road map of the southern environs of Oxford looking towards Dorchester-on-Thames would be helpful, though perhaps not essential. You will look in vain for Littlemore on a railway map of the present day.

Numerous towns and villages throughout the country have become show places, visited by tourists and coach excursions and constantly photographed. Some are subjects for painters, professional and amateur. Littlemore is not in that category. Neither is it one of those places which travel writers delight to call "hidden" or "secret", or which are now noted for providing lavish mediaeval pageantry to attract visitors. All those developments are relatively recent. Littlemore has no need of them.

The village has not sought publicity. Arthur Mee, in his *King's England* volume on Oxfordshire (1949) wrote of Littlemore's past, but gave scarcely any information on the place itself. This is not in the least disparaging. Surely it is good to enjoy the unspectacular, away from crowds; all England was like that once. For us it is not a question of retreating into the past, even though we may regret many modern developments, not least the destruction of our villages and their traditions, the imposition of alien cultures and the loss of much that we valued. Nostalgia is a powerful force, but few of us would truthfully want to settle in the 1840s, although in Littlemore we might then have seen and known some remarkable men, of unquenchable influence, who were drawn to this village.

It must be admitted that proximity to Oxford shaped the history of Littlemore at that time and since. It could hardly be otherwise. There was always "Oxford and the countryside and the river and the sun that rises over Wadham and sets over Worcester", in the memorable words of an Oxford scholar of a later generation, Mgr Ronald Knox. Although linked to Oxford, it was not *in* Oxford. The charm of Littlemore lay partly in its rural character and independence; it was still in the country, as is evident from old prints, several of which are reproduced in these pages. Littlemore is marked on Thomas Moule's County map, first published in 1830, where it is spelt Littlemoor, in the Hundred of Bullington.

To trace Littlemore's remote, earthy origin need not take long. Geologically it is situated on the Oxford Plain. When it began to be inhabited is not known. The place-name is not encouraging[1]. It is thought to mean simply a small marsh or moor (mōr), suggesting a bleak, even barren landscape; anciently, not an attractive place to live, yet people settled there.

A brief description of Littlemore as it has developed since then would be an Oxfordshire village lying mostly off the main road, about two-and-a-half miles south of Oxford. Its historic reputation rests almost exclusively on one man, whose *residence* there lasted no more than four years (1842-46), yet Littlemore will always be associated with him. That man was John Henry Newman, one of our finest Englishmen. Famous as an Anglican clergyman, he became even better known as a Roman Catholic priest. Littlemore stands as a pivot at the centre of his long life (1801-90).

Metaphorically we can approach Littlemore from Oxford, as Newman did. One writer who appreciated Oxford as a "Towery city and branchy between towers", also referred disparagingly to its "base and bricky skirt". In that class, no doubt, he included Littlemore. From a purely architectural point of view, such a description would fit many a village, suburb, or town, since most of our domestic building is of brick. The writer in question, Gerard Manley Hopkins (1844-89) the Jesuit poet, had no reason to love Littlemore. He did not know it intimately, as Newman did. Newman would look forward to its future potential, hesitantly, but with hope, seeing it as somewhere special, essential to the course of his life. Without the historical perspective, Littlemore *would* seem undistinguished - but don't be put off.

It is paradoxical that anyone coming to Littlemore will soon become aware of Newman, while readers of Newman biographies will already be aware of Littlemore as an essential stage on his life's journey. It would probably be true to say that without this association, Littlemore would have only a local interest today, in its own immediate neighbourhood, perhaps as a place for market gardening and normal country pursuits, or as a dormitory suburb of Oxford. As it is, 150 years later, it is a household word among historically-minded Anglicans and Catholics.

We are led to believe that the central features of most English villages are the church and the inn, established in that order. Here, it seems, is the unusual situation of the inns coming before the church, *unless* there was once a tiny ancient church which has disappeared completely, which is not an impossibility. There is nowhere for an archaeologist to dig, so no prospect of new finds. That does not alter our appreciation of Littlemore, of course. A place that can boast of much subterranean exploration is not necessarily a better place. Not everything can be measured by earth sciences. What then are we looking at in this (relatively) quiet corner of south Oxfordshire, close to the old county boundary with Berkshire? A town-planner's paradise? No. Neither is it recognisable as the marsh or moor that it is thought to have been in the distant past. Human habitation shows its cumulative effect; the wildness is gone, and what we see is something quite different.

A village without a village green and a pond it may be, but not lacking interest, even though the stocks are no longer in place and the older houses have been rebuilt. This is truly England, where history seems but yesterday. The scene is set for making a factual journey through time from then until now; but first we need to travel back several centuries before the nineteenth, when Littlemore presented a very different aspect. The map will not help much here.

Being no great distance from Dorchester, it must surely have been influenced by the untiring missionary efforts of St. Birinus, who was Bishop there in the 7th century. St. Bede the historian recorded of Birinus in A.D. 635 that "there [in Dorcic] he brought many people to God by his holy labours". Yet despite its episcopal status, Dorchester was never of larger size than a village, so we cannot expect Littlemore to have been more than a small settlement in Anglo-Saxon times. Being remote from the coast, its inhabitants were not greatly troubled by foreign invaders arriving from the continent, but it was not easy being a Christian in those unsettled times.

Early history is seldom as coherent as we would like and there are bound to be some gaps in our knowledge; certainly so before the Normans brought the manorial system to England.

It seems clear that around the time of the Norman invasion Littlemore was of no importance, since it does not appear in the Domesday survey of 1085-86. From this it can be assumed that whatever the population, it was neither extensive nor wealthy in terms of land ownership and farm stock. Perhaps a few peasants eked out a modest living. There may have been fishing in the Thames at Sandford and probably some forms of hunting. The people would not have gone hungry, even if they had little variety in their food and not a great deal of excitement in their lives. Oxford would have provided some diversion for the able-bodied who could find their way on foot or horseback, and also opportunities for trading. Cottage industries may have begun to develop. The population is likely to have grown steadily, at least until the Black Death.

Having introduced Littlemore, we come now to rather more tangible history. "Then" becomes nearer, as the centuries recede, uneventfully perhaps.

1

St. Nicholas Priory, the Mynchery

There seems no reason to suppose that in mediaeval times Littlemore was especially prosperous or significant. It was not directly on one of the major pilgrimage or trade routes, so it would have been largely by-passed. The growing fame of Oxford, its University and numerous religious houses, would have attracted talent and wealth to itself. However, there was one convent in the locality extant in the thirteenth century. This was the Priory of St. Nicholas, a small community of Benedictine nuns, founded by Robert de Sandford, who was Master of the Knights Templar in England *circa* 1229-48.

The Knights Templar of the nearby Sandford Preceptory[2], to whom the Manor of Littlemore was granted *circa* 1235, were the patrons of St. Nicholas Priory *circa* 1240-1312. Unfortunately, it acquired a bad name around 1445, when there were seven nuns in the convent. Thereafter, it continued to go downhill morally, and never recovered. In 1517, the community consisted of only six nuns, who seem to have been a most undisciplined lot. Their reputation did not attract new vocations and could not be allowed to continue. (We can only hope that the villagers were of a higher calibre.) The Priory's net income in 1524 was *circa* £33. The conclusion of this travesty came when St. Nicholas Priory was finally dissolved by Cardinal Wolsey in 1525, the proceeds being applied to his new foundation, Cardinal College in Oxford (later to be known as Christ Church). Minchery Farm was built on the site of the Priory. Following the usual practice of the time, most of the old stonework was incorporated into the farm buildings which were altered by later owners.

11

Minchery Farm is now served by Oxford Transport, which passes through Littlemore. It should be explained that the word "mynchery" (i.e. nunnery) derived from the Old English *myncen* meaning "a nun". The distinctive name of the property, old even in the mid-sixteenth century, remained after the nuns departed. It is clear that by the time Eliza J. Burton made her sketch in 1845 only a few displaced fragments of stonework which survived from the Priory were thought worthy of note.

The Priory church was rebuilt in the 13th century and the eastern range of the convent buildings, with the dormitory above, was probably rebuilt in the mid-15th century, owing to its ruinous condition *circa* 1445. The nuns derived a certain amount of income from various properties in Oxford and also from boarding children.

The Priory's corporate seal[3] was Gothic in design, within a pointed oval, and represented the patron St. Nicholas, Bishop of Myra, kneeling in prayer between two angels with censers. This would not have been an unusual form of seal for a convent.

Much else is no longer visible, through the wastage of time and changes of user. All the more remarkable, then, that the name subsists. The Mynchery it was and the Mynchery it remains, whether or not its derivation is remembered, or even cared about. We know a little about the appearance of the grounds from later visitors. The Mynchery was said to have "been formerly well wooded and its walks and devout recesses shaded with pleasant arbours. Many fish ponds have been there..." some of which remained in 1661, when those words were written. Hearne, who visited the farm in February 1722, writing his impressions of what he saw, mentioned that "there is a little stream that runs on the west side of the house, that they call the brook, but was formerly called the Rhee. So that Minchery ... may properly be called Nun Brook." As a tributary, this stream "falleth into the Isis by Sandford", that is, *away* from Littlemore.

An "old table at which the nuns used to dine" was used in the late eighteenth century at harvest homes and sheep shearings in the locality. That tells us something about the traditional way of life in an age when sheep farming was more widespread than now.

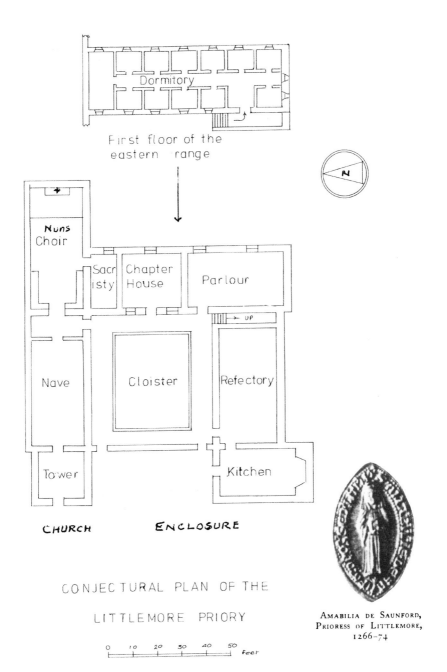

First floor of the
eastern range

N

Nuns
Choir

Sacr
isty

Chapter
House

Parlour

UP

Nave

Cloister

Refectory

Tower

Kitchen

CHURCH   ENCLOSURE

CONJECTURAL PLAN OF THE

LITTLEMORE PRIORY

0   10   20   30   40   50
                        Feet

AMABILIA DE SAUNFORD,
PRIORESS OF LITTLEMORE,
1266-74

13

Littlemore has no houses of special architectural interest like those of North Hinksey which were commended by John Ruskin (before his insanity). With no royal patronage, no eccentric residents or serious scandals since 1525, Littlemore could be classed as an ordinary rural area populated by ordinary people. Continuing in this rather negative vein, there is little that is mediaeval or pre-Reformation to be seen intact today, though several of the older houses survive, the most senior being Corpus Christi Farmhouse, dating from *circa* 1430. Before the 1840s it had been just a sleepy hamlet out in the country, not a parish with its own church; a place not much esteemed by Oxford men until one of them, the Vicar of St. Mary the Virgin, the University Church, sensing its potential decided to provide a church for the people of Littlemore, which he did.

Before 1835 services had been held in borrowed premises. These were known as "cottage services". Then it was decided that sufficient people were attending to justify something more permanent, which was an important milestone in the story of Littlemore. A rough calculation, probably inadequate, placed the population in 1831 at about 200. Presumably only a fraction of that number attended the cottage services. Some may have been attached to St. Andrew's Church, Sandford-on-Thames, the next parish to Littlemore.

A Baptist Chapel had been erected in 1804, which would have accounted for some of the regular worshippers.

The Seal of Littlemore Priory

2

A New Planting

Littlemore came into history almost accidentally, so it would seem; unexpectedly would be truer, since these events were not accidents.

In 1828 the Revd John Henry Newman accepted the prestigious living of St. Mary the Virgin, Oxford, a largely non-residential parish closely identified with the University, with which went the cure of souls in Littlemore, where he saw the possibilities of fruitful development. In February of the following year he began evening classes for the people there, his Sunday "Evening Catechetical Lectures". This was the beginning of changes. For the next fourteen years he was actively concerned for the well-being of Littlemore and its inhabitants, an aspect of his life often overlooked. While he was vicar of the University Church, his heart was with his people in Littlemore. By all accounts he flung himself more and more into parish work there - his catechising of the children became famous and men went out from Oxford on Sundays to hear it, when few Anglican clergy were noted for their pastoral zeal.

The success of this ministry accentuated the need for a permanent church building as soon as possible. Cottage services were outgrown and it was not feasible to expect the very young and the elderly to walk a distance to church in all weathers. A subscription list was opened. A number of Newman's friends were among those who responded and sufficient funds were raised, though not without some anxiety. Nothing in the Littlemore story came easily.

At what is now the junction of Sandford Road and Cowley Road was an undeveloped site, of a size suitable for the new church. When this site was cleared ready for building to commence, in 1836, some human remains were found on either side, suggesting the existence of an earlier graveyard thereabouts, either Christian or pagan. Archaeology not having achieved its present popularity, no investigation was made into this. In any case it was necessary to press on with the building. Funds were limited and time precious; so we know nothing about when those earlier burials took place, or why this area was chosen.

The plans went ahead and the church was duly erected, though not, as we shall see, fully completed until years later, when there was not the same urgency. These were still early years for the Oxford Movement, in which Newman was a central figure, so caution and prudence were essential if secure progress was to be made.

REMAINS OF THE MYNCHERY, LITTLEMORE
(*Pencil sketch by Eliza Burton, in possession of Miss R. M. Marshall*)

16

3

Trees and Stone: a Time for Building

Newman's experiences of Oxford colleges had given him a liking for some form of community life which he never lost. It seems that he had in view a monastic house, not a popular idea at that time. For this purpose in 1840 he "bought 10 acres of ground and began planting; but this great design was never carried out". The time was not ripe for such an experiment within the Church of England and it occasioned some suspicion. The prejudices of those days seem very curious and old-fashioned to us now.

Nineteenth-century opinions differ about Littlemore as about many things. Matthew Arnold (1822-88), an Oxford graduate, writing from memory, described it as a "dreary village". Then it mainly consisted of houses built of rubble with thatched roofs, a lane branching off from the village road and a blacksmith's forge for the making of horse-shoes and farm implements; hardly an idyllic picture, but not unpleasant. The bleak, neglected landscape was so transformed by the tree-planting begun by Newman that it could no longer be called dreary. In 1868 he could write, "Littlemore is now green", which makes him one of the first practical environmentalists, although he was not a countryman by birth.

For Newman, Littlemore was the favourite part of his parish (and the most responsive), where he was among friends who appreciated him and as time passed, it became a place of tender memories. So much began in those years which would come to fruition later; perhaps, in unexpected ways, *much* later. The interest shown in Littlemore was bound to make it more prosperous, materially as well as spiritually.

H. Graves, B.A., captain of the Oxford University Bicycle Club 1893-94, summed up Littlemore, as he knew it around that time, in a few sentences as:

> A pleasant little village, the church of which was one of the first productions of the revived school of Gothic architecture. The windows (by Willement) are worth inspection.
>
> Littlemore is well known as the scene of the labours of Newman and Pusey[4], to the former of whom is due the foundation of the church. A farmhouse was converted into sets of rooms for their followers and it was hence were issued the famous *Tracts for the Times*, which not only brought into existence the modern High Church party, but did much to rouse the whole Church into a healthy activity, of which we are today feeling the effects.
>
> *The Way About Oxfordshire* (no date)

Mr Graves, though sparing of words, was clearly expressing approval of those labours.

The church to which he referred bears the traditionally English dedication jointly to St. Mary and St. Nicholas[5]. The architect was Henry Jones Underwood (1804-52) of Oxford. Built in 1836, it was a small, unpretentious building, rectangular in shape and had at first neither chancel nor aisles. Since then it has been substantially altered and enlarged to fuller proportions, so that we do not see it exactly as it was then. It may be said to have grown gradually to its present dimensions.

As noted above, his church which was consecrated by Dr Richard Bagot, Bishop of Oxford, on 22 September 1836, actually began its existence as a Chapel of Ease dependent upon St. Mary the Virgin,

Oxford. In fact Littlemore remained part of St. Mary's parish until 1847 when it became a separate parish. In 1848 the chancel and north-east tower were added at the expense of Mr Crawley, a local benefactor. The architect on this occasion was J. Clarke. His tower was intended to support a spire but this was never completed, remaining as a square tower like those of so many Oxfordshire churches, e.g. Black Bourton and Brize Norton.

In common with most churches, the interior decoration was added to over the years. At first it was extremely plain. The Rood figures were carved at Oberammergau and presented to the church in 1901, by an American donor, to mark the centenary of Newman's birth. The screen, designed by F. H. Crossley, was erected in 1913. The font, of thirteenth-century workmanship, came from the mother-church in Oxford, the cover being added in 1924. The lead lining is original.

On the north wall of the nave the monument to the vicar's mother, Mrs Jemima Newman (1836), by a family friend, the noted sculptor Richard Westmacott Jnr., R.A., is of historic interest. She had laid the foundation stone of the church in the previous year, on 21 July 1835, and died the following May. The windows of Newman's church were at first of plain transparent glass, except for a single red pane at the east end. Then in the 1840s came the glass by Thomas Willement (or Williment) which Mr Graves deemed "worth inspection". Some of it has since been replaced. The north-east and south-east windows of the nave have single figures set in clear glass by William Morris's firm, Morris & Co., in 1887.

Littlemore Church has been described more recently as "tall and depressing, with great bat-wing roof timbers"; perhaps fair comment, though it should be remembered that the building was restricted by funds available, raised by public subscription. Even an architect like A W N Pugin was all too familiar with the problems caused by shortage of money. The so-called Gothic Revival provided the obvious choice in the circumstances - a building of simple honest dignity.

In fairness, we cannot compare a nineteenth-century village church to a mediaeval college chapel. Doubtless the inhabitants of Littlemore were proud of their church and thankful for it. As Newman himself said years later, "It was a glad time when we first met here". One (unnamed) man is reported to have said if he could but live to be buried in Littlemore churchyard, he should die happy. Here was a place which strongly attracted different types of people. Even if no-one would mistake this church for a mediaeval building, or for the work of Pugin[6], it was commendable, genuinely "Christian architecture", very much the Oxford style of the period and generally well appreciated. The architect may not have made his fortune, but his church here has achieved a certain unlooked-for immortality.

A long account of the Consecration Service which appeared in an Oxford newspaper included the following information:

> The whole east end of the interior, in particular, is in the style of better days, and can hardly fail to remind every thoughtful spectator of the solemn purposes to which it is devoted. We understand, and it is most important that all who are connected with the erection of new Churches should know, that the total expense of this most beautiful structure, including every extra, fell something short of £800.

This may seem to us somewhat ambiguous. Was the writer commenting favourably on the builders' careful economy, or was he hinting that other church builders might cost more?

As will be seen, the vicar was keen on enlivening the services musically, teaching the children to sing and to chant the psalms. The singing of hymns was at first accompanied by a barrel organ, then fashionable, but obviously restricting the choice of tunes; those available were likely to be over-played. Evidently the "extras" did not include a pipe organ (which would then have been a luxury for a small church).

The "wooden eagle for the Bible" presented by a donor, cost £30; an interesting example of a carved wooden lectern in an age when ecclesiastical brassware was in the ascendent.

Being an entirely new building, on virgin soil so to speak, there was nothing old to be incorporated into its structure. The architect had a free hand in designing a church conventional and practicable, with no inkling of how his work would be judged and known in the future. As a contemporary of Pugin he was clearly open to the same influences, though his work here was necessarily on a more modest scale, without needless ornament.

As regards the windows, with our later familiarity with so much glass of a finer standard, these do not seem memorable examples. However, that is not a fair criterion, for stained glass-making had passed through a long period of mediocrity and Willement was considered a fine craftsman. There was sufficient daylight in the church, but, apart from flowers and greenery at festivals like Easter (as mentioned in 1840), there was little colour. Vestments were not yet in use.

As might be expected, having regard to the later developments of the Oxford Movement, the church would have looked more austere (and certainly smaller) in Newman's incumbency than now. It was always dignified, but much has been done to beautify the interior since.

Besides the windows, Willement is also thought to have designed the reredos. One item of historical interest which should not be missed is the list of subscribers to the original building which includes some prominent names. This is to be found on the west wall of the nave. Unlike some older churches in Oxfordshire, Littlemore has never been noted for bell-ringing, there being only one bell. This bell was nevertheless strangely immortalised in 1845, as will be related.

There are in existence a number of drawings of the exterior of the new church dating from around this time. In one of these, an engraving by F. B. Delt of Littlemore Church from the west, 1838, the stocks are plainly visible by the roadside as a warning to offenders. They would have pre-dated the church. It is a fact that the stocks remained in general use in England as a public punishment for civil offences until about the mid-nineteenth century, though there was an isolated case of their use in Newbury as late as 1872. Littlemore's stocks disappeared to an unknown destination, but that was not the end of the story. The old stocks having gone, a new set was made in 1857 by Richard Humphries, who was the village carpenter and constable, especially for the punishment of a man sentenced to six hours in the stocks. In such a public place as College Lane, he would have been seen by all and probably mocked by some, but once released, his offence could be forgotten.

Those early pictures give a taste of the exposed bleakness of the site around the church which Matthew Arnold remembered so dismally, before such developments as the churchyard, the school, and newly-planted trees improved the scene. What had been leafless became living; natural life re-introduced. The species of trees favoured by Newman were "larch and fir with more tender trees, yet suited to the soil, such as hornbeam, &c." Littlemore today is not prolifically wooded[7], rather less than he would have liked. Had he stayed the rest of his life here as a country parson, doubtless more trees would have grown. Later on he wrote of "the Summer wind among the lofty pines", but that was hardly reminiscent of Littlemore.

LITTLEMORE CHURCH. OXON.

Londen by J. H. Brown, Oxford

LITTLEMORE CHURCH
Coloured engraving at Magdalen College

Engraving of the church in 1838 by F.B. Delt

22

4

Lessons for Learning

Although the vicar was still living in Oxford after the new church was opened, he decided that it was in Littlemore he was "to pass the Lent of 1840 ... teaching in the Parish School and practising the choir". English church choirs and their music were at a low ebb when the Tractarians started to revive the quality of worship. Littlemore led the way in this, and training the children from an early age was vitally important. Newman was an educator throughout his life and we can be sure of one thing - he did not waste time. The children received a good, wholesome foundation which they would never forget.

Village schools have not always been treated kindly by writers, but seldom have the teachers been of the academic and spiritual standard of Newman. In the circumstances he had to devise his own methods, trying out what best suited his pupils. Although it was not an easy start - the schoolmistress was unsatisfactory and addicted to drinking - we have the impression, from his own words, that his teaching worked well and produced results.

During that Lent he was gratified that "the children are vastly improved in singing", but admitted that "there is much to be done at the school". We get an all too brief glimpse of the school from a letter Newman wrote to his sister about the progress made with the children, especially relating to the singing lessons:

I have had the audacity to lead them and teach them some new tunes. Also I have rummaged out a violin and strung it, and on Mondays and Thursdays have begun to *lead* with it a party of between 20 and 30, great and little, in the school room. Moreover, I have begun chanting - and by way of experiment, a Gregorian chant, which the children seem to take to, though they have not learned it yet - for, I see, it makes them smile - though that may be at me.

I am catechising them in Church too, and have got them on so far, that they take *interest* in it. But I am sadly off for girls. I have only one, I suppose, as much as 10 - and not two more than 8 or 9, except some Sunday Scholars, who have not time to learn what I would teach them.

I have effected a great reform (for the time) in the girls' hands and faces - lectured with unblushing effrontery on the necessity of *keeping their work clean* and set them to knit stockings with all their might. Also, I am going to give them some neat white pinafores for Church use, and am going to contrive to make them make them ...

Also I have drawn up a sort of liturgy of school prayers varying with the seasons ... and mean to have them hung up in the schoolroom and used according to the day.

The little school building, shown in the caricature sketch, adjacent to the church, must have been overcrowded at times. The eminent teacher, if, for those days, unorthodox in his methods, was certainly getting results. He himself began to learn the violin when he was a schoolboy of ten.

That same year (1840) he spent Easter at Littlemore, and wrote on that day: "We are all so happy that we are afraid of being too happy; we have got some roses, wallflowers, and sweet briar, and the Chapel smells as if to remind one of the Holy Sepulchre." This atmosphere contrasted with that of St. Mary's, which Newman always found so cold and unresponsive. (The chapel was the new church, which was still officially a chapel within the Oxford parish at that time.)

The day school had been provided through the efforts of the Revd J. R. Bloxam while he was curate (1837-40). The architect, Henry Underwood, had also designed the church, resulting in the building being compatible in style. The land on which the school was built cost £25, rather less than the lectern in the church! Without attempting comparison with present day prices, it would seem that land prices were not unduly high, there being no shortage of land here, when Littlemore was beginning to grow.

From what we know of his personal life it seems that Newman was always a plain living man, not fond of luxury. The thought of living on the fat of the land did not appeal to him. He was no hunting/shooting parson, devoting much time to a round of social activities and heavy drinking, as had been the case in many country parishes. All that was slowly changing. Littlemore's church life was evolving healthily with so conscientious a pastor instructing the children and their parents, doing all that he could to help them. What came to be known as the Oxford Movement was gathering momentum; Littlemore played a valuable part, quietly pointing the way forward.

Writing to his sister, Harriett, Newman told her of his longing for a little parish away from the busy world; his wish was for solitude in a quiet, domestic setting, perhaps like his friend the Revd John Keble. This he found for a while at Littlemore, with his books and music to help. In fact his years here formed but a small fraction of his long life, yet Littlemore meant much to him.

Littlemore never knew him as an old man. It was in his early forties that he could be seen almost daily, energetically "striding along the Oxford Road ..." about his varied ministry, or travelling at greater speed on horseback.

Among the advantages of Littlemore was its proximity to Oxford and Newman's friends in the University; yet at the same time it was separate enough to enable him to withdraw into a different society where life was less sophisticated. He was thoroughly in his element here, delighting in the simplicity of village life and enjoying his pastoral work. There was a world of difference between the people here and the "critics and carpers" whom he encountered at St. Mary's, Oxford. Our knowledge of those days relies mainly on items of correspondence which have been preserved.

The tempo of life followed a regular pulse, set by nature. People were used to working hard to earn a living from agriculture and fared none the worse for it. A man such as the blacksmith would have been kept busy at his trade. Bloxam, during his short curacy, lodged with him, in the rooms which Newman later occupied for a while, around 1841.

In the drawing of Littlemore *circa* 1840 showing the Oxford Road, the George and Dragon inn can be seen, marked by a free-standing inn sign of St George. Next door stood the blacksmith's forge and house, then occupied by Mr and Mrs George Barnes. (There could hardly have been anything more traditionally English; travellers could have enjoyed a drink while the blacksmith and the ostler attended to the horses' needs.) The road here was pleasantly green with trees, giving an illusion of being more isolated than it was even then. The George is thought to date from 1766 as a coaching inn. Such was the demand for the blacksmith's craft in the heyday of the coach and horses that there were no less than three smithies working. One of these continued to exist until 1924.

Littlemore had no need of street lighting as road traffic posed no great problems. Unless one had a horse, the usual mode of transport locally was either on foot or by a one horse vehicle known as a "fly". Newman himself was a good horseman. While living at Oriel, like every resident Fellow (unless infirm), he kept a horse, a spirited mare called Klepper, well known in Littlemore. She had Arab blood in her and was considered dangerous to an unskilled rider.

Bicycles had not yet taken over the streets of Oxford. The young men from the University doubtless walked to Littlemore, enjoying the exercise and each other's company on the way. The only large vehicles would have been the stage coach at its appointed times along the main road and a heavy old farm cart trundling by, at a less urgent pace. Given favourable weather the coach made a brave show dashing along the road to or from Oxford, but on a stormy day the passengers could expect an unpleasant ride.

The construction of the roads was not ideal, though they served a useful purpose of communication. Made of flint and sand, they were dusty in summer and muddy in winter. The footpaths were gravel.

Interior of the church, looking eastward, as it was in Newman's time. From a sepia sketch of 1839.

CARICATURE SKETCH OF THE SCHOOL, CHURCH, AND MR. NEWMAN'S BUILDINGS ("PRIORY") AT LITTLEMORE IN 1844.

5

Autumn: the Parting of Friends

There was a sense of satisfaction and an air of optimistic progress; perhaps the incipient stirrings of a "Second Spring"? Even the growing trees which Newman had commenced planting "near the highway from Sandford to Oxford", that is, along the main road, were a sign of renewal. Yet, as the story unfolds, it is clear that Littlemore has autumn associations; not only a matter of falling leaves, of which it has no monopoly, but rather the autumnal fulfilment of one work and the transition to another, giving a sense of sadness tempered with the promise of a new spring to come. The world of nature interacts with the spiritual in a way which both poets and theologians appreciate. Newman was both.

He was not destined to spend the rest of his life ministering in Oxford and Littlemore, but at the right moment would leave his adopted county, which meant so much to him. That time was not yet. For a while, life here seemed to have permanence and good prospects. In April 1842 he wrote of moving into his "new abode at Littlemore" and his dream of what might come of it, if all went well:

> I have long wished to live at Littlemore and the difficulty has been to get a room for a library. Last Spring the heirs of old Costar turned a granary into a number of cottages, and I offered to rent them, on condition of their turning a stable which adjoined into a room (for books) .... I have taken my books there, and shall care little whether I get other inmates

besides myself or not. Perhaps my curate will come - perhaps
my school-master - perhaps my Secretary- perhaps some
village boy who can be made something of - perhaps one or
two pupils - perhaps some Oxford friends.

He had hopes of a simple community of men with a rule which would
draw them together as a family in useful service. There seemed to be
scope for such a project. It was a wonderful dream.

However, as the next year ripened into autumn his ministry as an
Anglican clergyman reached its conclusion. For reasons of conscience
he could not continue. Soon that familiar voice would no longer be heard
there in church and schoolroom. He had no quarrel with Littlemore, nor
as yet any wish to depart from there; indeed, before resigning his living he
had tried to keep Littlemore for himself, "even though it was still to remain
an integral part of St Mary's". This request was not granted, so his
resignation applied to both churches. Ironically the parish was later divided.

Many country churches are filled for the Harvest Thanksgiving,
but in the early 1840s this annual event had not become widely established,
yet some of its elements were anticipated in the course of a sermon
remembered now for other reasons. It was the vicar's last message to his
flock after serving them for fifteen years. Not an easy occasion, with so
many friends gathered from all walks of life listening attentively. This, one
of the most memorable sermons, on "The Parting of Friends", was
preached at Littlemore on Monday 25 September 1843, for the
anniversary of the church's dedication. It had unique quality as the last
act of Newman's ministry there and was a sorrowful occasion for the
friends who worshipped in his little church, now full of flowers - dahlias,
fuchsias and passion flowers. He spoke of "certain circumstances" of
the season and time, in fine clear English, linking them to the Bible and the
Church's calendar:

> For now are the shades of evening falling upon the earth,
> and the year's labour is coming to its end. In Septuagesima
> the labourers were sent into the vineyard; in Sexagesima the
> sower went forth to sow; that time is over; 'the harvest is

NEWMAN'S BUILDING AT LITTLEMORE:
Intended to form the nucleus of a monastic house.

passed, the summer is ended'; the vintage is gathered. We have kept the Ember-days for the fruits of the earth … now we are offering up of its corn and wine as a propitiation, and are eating and drinking of them with thanksgiving.

This theme gave place to another, less welcome, because no-one enjoys partings. In the last paragraph of this long sermon he commended himself (in the third person) to the "kind and affectionate hearts" of his hearers, asking them to "remember such a one in time to come, though you hear him not …" (Sermon 26). It was an oblique farewell, in keeping with the gentle humility of the preacher. His message was not lost on his hearers.

How did this event affect the inhabitants of Littlemore? To some it must have seemed odd and rather puzzling why Mr Newman retreated from the church where he had ministered to them and then shut himself away at the other end of the street. Whether they appreciated his motives or not, they knew that he must follow his conscience. It had always been so - "one step enough for me". Daily life would continue, tinged with a certain sadness. This autumn was a feast of bitter herbs.

His present action was clear enough, the course of his life in the future was yet uncertain, an uncharted voyage, but he was not suddenly leaving Littlemore. For another two years he lived there quietly with his friends, withdrawn from parochial work, preparing for the next step. They adopted a quasi-monastic style of life, living in simple comfort, with no hint of luxury or utopianism, perhaps (while not intending it) making reparation for the long past misdemeanours of the Priory. Simplicity of living accorded well with the rural character of Littlemore in the 1840s. Sleeping on a straw mattress and undertaking rigorous fasts and penances, it was a much harder life than that of the average countryman. The local people would doubtless have been horrified at the self-imposed austerity practised in the College, as detailed in Newman's private journal. Though living as a strict community, they were not bound by vows and this experiment was not a religious order as such. It is of interest as pointing forward to his Oratorian life in Birmingham.

A contemporary drawing of Newman, out walking.

Littlemore is remarkably compact. Only a hundred yards north of the church stands the College, as can be seen in an old print, where it is curiously named "Priory" (which it never was)[8]. Notice that the signpost pointing to Oxford was altered to Oscott by the mischievous artist. Precisely when the College first came by its present name is not certain. Though not the most impressive of buildings architecturally, this is one of the focal points for the serious visitor. As will be seen, the buildings have had a varied history through the nineteenth century until our own time.

However much Littlemore may have been built up since Newman's time (as it obviously has been), we can still see where he lived with his few companions. The row of cottages or tenements has been variously identified as formerly a farmhouse or farm cottages, or possibly a converted stable block, though in 1842 Newman clearly stated that it had then been a granary with a stable adjoining. There may well have been a number of changes of user in the past. The Italian Passionist Father Dominic (referred to later) wrote of it as "a building which has more the look of a barn than a dwellinghouse - divided so as to form so many little cells". As a monk he naturally thought that way. Strongly built to last many winters, it has remained a familiar sight, old, but not crumbling away.

The building bears the name "college" in a mediaeval sense, meaning a community of religious persons living under a rule (e.g. a college of priests), rather than a place of education for students like an Oxford college within the University. It never had this status. There was no outward organisation, since the college at Littlemore did not exist for that reason. It was more a private haven or retreat for its own inhabitants, a character which today permeates it more strongly than the original rural use, whatever its precise function. Living here must have seemed very quiet after Oxford, a contrast which proportionately still holds good.

Perhaps the villagers passing by in the afternoon may sometimes have heard Mr Newman playing his violin, by way of solace and relaxation (well before the invention of radio!) He also played Beethoven[9] and Haydn sonatas with a pianist friend in the schoolroom; somewhat different to his leading the school children's singing a few years back. He was a master of English and all his life engaged in writing and correspondence, not least at Littlemore where he could find peace to concentrate; a temporary peace, for Newman could not remain here indefinitely in this pleasant seclusion. He was never a solitary. Equipped with an ink-bottle and quill pen, he wrote standing at a high desk, which can still be seen in the College.

The old country saying "early to bed, early to rise ..." certainly applied to the life there (though they could not expect to be made "wealthy"!) Probably other early risers were going about their work even earlier. Waking by the sun rather than by an alarm clock has always come naturally to those in tune with the seasons. A sample of local occupations can be gathered from the Baptismal Register for the year 1836-37, the first year that the church was open. Among the fathers listed were a papermaker, a baker, a cornfactor (or chandler?) and a number of labourers, unspecified; all manual workers, men whose families were settled here and who seldom travelled far afield.

A watercolour "Hay-making at Littlemore", one of a series of local studies by Emma D. Herschel (and now belonging to the Bodelian Library at Oxford), shows the hay-makers at work, seemingly very close to the west end of the church, which was by then complete with its tower. Assuming the authenticity of this scene, Littlemore must still have been truly agricultural during Newman's tenure here and for some years thereafter.

All the usual rural employment could be found in Littlemore, not only agricultural work. As long ago as 1611, malting was a subsidiary occupation in Cowley Road. However we do not hear that a market was held. Littlemore developed like any other village, its most important shop being the Post Office and General Stores, which sold nearly everything.

Baptisms Solemnized in the Parish of St. Mary and St. Nicholas, Littlemore
In the County of Oxford — In the Year 1836-37

1836						
Sept. 22nd (born Aug. 31) No. 1	Anne	John and Eliza	Castles	Littlemore	Papermaker	John H. Newman Vicar
Sept. 22nd. (born Sept. 7) No. 2	Harriet	John and Mary Anne	Haynes	Littlemore	Baker	John H. Newman Vicar
Nov. 13th. No. 3	Dinah	William and Sarah	Cordery	Littlemore	Labourer	I. Williams Minister
Nov. 20th. (born Nov. 6) No. 4	Martha	John and Sarah	Stimpson	Littlemore	Labourer	I. Williams
Dec. 11th. No. 5	Mary Anne	Henry and Anne	Parsons	Littlemore	Labourer	C. L. Cornish Off. Minister
Dec. 25th. (born Dec. 2) No. 6	Sarah	Richard and Mary	Bampton	Littlemore	Labourer	Is. Williams Off. Minister
1837						
Feb. 26th. (born Jan. 10) No. 7	Christopher	Charles and Sophia	Honey	Littlemore	Cornfactor	C. L. Cornish Off. Minister
Feb. 26th. (born Feb. 17) No. 8	Elizabeth	John and Mary	Whiting	Littlemore	Labourer	Is. Williams Off. Minister

6

Another Autumn: the Decision Taken

In the autumn of 1845 matters swiftly came to a head. Monday 8 October was the crucial date. In the College there was a sense of quiet expectation and urgency. Newman sat down in his room and wrote some thirty letters to his friends and relatives, telling them of his decision: before the letters were posted, he would have been received into the Roman Catholic Church. For some it would be a second "Parting of Friends".

The dramatic events of that stormy night 150 years ago have often been recounted; the meeting of two remarkable men at Littlemore (both commemorated here). Even the elements of nature seemed to underline its obscurity, yet it could not be hidden. Even without the modern media the world would know of Littlemore and what happened there, making the village famous beyond scholars' dreams. Father Dominic Barberi, travelling from Aston and passing through Oxford and London to Belgium, was persuaded to make a detour to visit Littlemore. A foreign visitor arriving at night would, perhaps, be enough to set the villagers talking and speculating on his business with Mr Newman, in the circumstances.

Father Dominic, who arrived in Oxford on the stage coach, was then escorted to Littlemore in pouring rain by two of Newman's companions. Arriving soaked to the skin he was put by the fire to dry out. (That will always be remembered!) The sequel was, for many people, a foregone conclusion. Newman had at last reached the point of changing his spiritual allegiance. So it was that his admission into the Catholic Church took place not in a great church or a distant monastery, but in this homely setting in a corner of south Oxfordshire; the familiar, not "the distant scene".

Drawing of Littlemore Church, based on an illustration
by Mr Walsh, a former inhabitant. The original is now in the possession of the
Littlemore PCC.

To appreciate the impact on Littlemore, we need to look back some hours earlier. A contemporary, the Revd Frederick Oakeley, wrote a fine graphic description of that "memorable day" (tracing it from the morning). It is worth quoting at length.

> The rain came down in torrents, bringing with it the first heavy instalment of autumn's "sere and yellow" leaves. The wind, like a spent giant, howled forth the expiring notes of its equinoctial fury. The superstitious might have said that the very elements were on the side of Anglicanism, so copiously did they weep, so piteously bemoan, the approaching departure of its great representative. The bell which swung visibly in the turret of the little Gothic church at Littlemore gave that day the usual notice of morning and afternoon prayers; but it came to the ear in that buoyant, bouncing tone which is usual in a high wind, and sounded more like a knell than a summons. The "monastery" was more than usually sombre and still. Egress and ingress there was none that day, for it had been given out ... that "Mr Newman wished to remain quiet".

So the day

> passed off without producing any satisfaction to the general curiosity. All that transpired was that a remarkable-looking man, evidently a foreigner, and shabbily dressed in black, had asked his way to Mr Newman's ...

F. Oakeley, *The Tractarian Movement*

There seems some discrepancy here, though the precise circumstance of Father Dominic's arrival is not of any great historical importance. In either case, we can understand the reactions of the local people, who were mostly long-standing friends of Mr Newman (and who would always remember him); though respecting his privacy, they were keen to satisfy their natural curiosity, just as we would have been. They did not have to wait long.

Outwardly, the only difference to be seen was that instead of going to services in St Mary and St Nicholas, Newman, with several fellow converts, now attended a small Catholic chapel in Oxford. The establishment lost interest in Littlemore and its former vicar.

He was conscious that a part of his life - that associated with the Church of England and Littlemore - had come to an end and he recognised that it was almost time to move on. Otherwise he might have drifted into a scholarly backwater. In fact he stayed some months longer, settling outstanding matters and preparing for the next step. Of necessity the property would have to be sold when he left.

Littlemore was certainly a harbour and a bower, a place of shelter from life's storms. Newman thought of it that way when on 20 January 1846 he wrote to a friend: "I realise more that we are leaving Littlemore and it is like going on the open sea." *(Apologia pro Vita Sua)* A month later he recalled, on Saturday 21 and Sunday 22 February 1846: "I was in my house at Littlemore simply by myself, as I had been for the first day or two when I had originally taken possession of it."

His companions had left; now he too was going away. Before leaving on the Sunday afternoon, he paused and, like many lesser men, admitted a moment of sentimentality: he kissed the bed, the mantelpiece and other parts of the house, because he had been happy there and noted, when packing and disposing all the different objects that had been part of his life, "passing from a metaphysical m/s to a lump of resin or an inkglass". This was his farewell, before tearing himself away from familiar scenes, and it was bound to be painful.

Very happy times have I had here, (though in much doubt) - and I am loth to leave it. Perhaps I shall never have quiet again - shall I ever see Littlemore again?

The question remained unanswered, but not altogether forgotten. Perhaps his former parishioners also wondered, when they reminisced on the dark winter evenings.

There is evidence enough for thinking that "leaving Littlemore evoked in Newman more regrets than leaving Oxford". He had not been at ease in the large and prestigious University Church; at Littlemore, all was different. He was closer to people who were not undergraduates or academics. Retrospectively he admitted to having been "happy at Oriel, happier at Littlemore ..." and so on. We have seen how it suited his temperament and he was not given to romancing about such things.

The College, as a quasi-monastic experiment (learning the hard way) never had any *official* existence or recognition, so the leasehold could be disposed of easily. Newman was not burdened with the property for years to come. That was by no means the end of the story, as we shall discover.

Inevitably, Newman's thoughts returned to Littlemore, not merely out of nostalgia, that would be natural enough. There was a deeper motive of personal gratitude. Writing to his friend, the Revd W. J. Copeland, soon after leaving Littlemore, he admitted that

"there it has been, that I have both been taught my way and received an answer to my prayers."

Letter dated 10 March 1846

It is evident that he still admired the so-called Gothic architecture with which he was familiar, for he wrote later that this style

is endowed with a profound and commanding beauty such as no other style possesses with which we are acquainted, and which probably the Church will not see surpassed till it attain to the Celestial City.

Dublin Discourses

In some small degree the Church of St. Mary and St. Nicholas must share in that tribute. Its simplified style (even when unfinished) was to exercise an influence on English churches built in the wake of the Oxford Movement. At one time it was intended to build a spire, but the plans had to be revised as the tower was not considered strong enough to support a spire.

The happenings of 1845, which had momentarily rocked the village consciousness, were receding. Scarcely four years later, the people of Littlemore would have heard the news that the mysterious visitor, Fr. Dominic, had died at Reading on 27 August 1849, while travelling by rail. At the age of 57, he was only nine years older than Newman, whose life was destined to reach into his ninetieth year. (This was not the last that Littlemore heard of Fr. Dominic's name.)

As we shall see, the Great Western Railway was at that time unknown in Littlemore, keeping the people to some extent isolated from the busy world until about 1864. In the meantime, Newman had been ordained in Rome and, having returned to England, founded the Oratory in a poor quarter of Birmingham. That was to be his permanent home, the embodiment of much that he had planned and longed for while living in Littlemore, the fruit of frustrated hopes.

However, as this is not intended to be yet another biography of him, but rather a study of Littlemore itself, we must not lose sight of the local scene; quietly industrious and not hitting the headlines, nor courting publicity (then or now).

Elevation of the Catholic Church of Bl. Dominic Barberi

Blessed Dominic, detail from a portrait.

An early view of the original station at Littlemore. *Pendon Museum*

Two views of Littlemore Station

An interesting shot of Littlemore which shows the signal box high up on the left hand embankment, and the Mental Hospital in the background, which was served by its own siding via a small wagon turntable. The earlier handcrane is also visible. *L & GRP*

7

The Railway Arrives

Years passed, and Littlemore, where he had once hoped to remain, still attracted Father Newman in his wholly different surroundings. This need not surprise us; it is never easy to sever the association of certain places, and although he became fond of his "nest" (or *nido*) at the Birmingham Oratory, he continued to look back with real affection to Littlemore. Sooner or later, the question would be answered in the affirmative.

There were bound to be changes, even in a small village. The environment is not static. By now the schoolchildren whom he had known and taught were grown up. Some would have moved away from home. Of the elderly, some had doubtless died, happy "to be buried in Littlemore churchyard". Social historians might speak of progress, with some justification; the railway had arrived. Steam trains rivalled the stage-coach and brought a new dimension to travel. Local men may have worked on the line.

These were certainly changes, but not surprises to a well-informed man. Essentially, Littlemore was as Newman remembered it. The easier access by rail seems likely to have influenced his decision, postponed for so long. More will be said later about the railway and how it affected Littlemore.

From a letter to Henry Wilberforce dated 18 June 1868, we learn that Father Newman indeed paid one more visit to Littlemore and expressed his satisfaction with all that he saw there. In the midst of his busy life in Birmingham he had not forgotten Littlemore and its country aspect:

45

I had always hoped to see it once before I died. Ambrose (Father Ambrose St John) and I went by the 7 a.m. train to Abingdon, then across to Littlemore - then direct from Littlemore by rail to Birmingham where we arrived by 7 - just 12 hours.

He then referred to tree planting:

At least I have begun something in that way at Littlemore, and Crawley has done as much again and much more tastefully. Littlemore is now *green*. Crawley's cottage and garden (upon my 10 acres which I sold him) are beautiful. The church too is now what they call a *gem*. And the parsonage is very pretty. I saw various of my people, now getting on in life. It was 40 years at the beginning of this year since I became vicar. Alas, their memory of me was in some cases stronger than my memory of them. They have a great affection for my Mother and Sisters[9] - tho' it is 32 years since they went away. There is a large lunatic asylum - separated, however, from the village by the railroad - so it is no annoyance, rather it adds green to the place - nor is the railroad an annoyance, for it is in a cutting. It is 22 years since I was there ... I do not expect ever to see it again - nor do I wish it.

On this occasion the circumstances were different and less dramatic; it was not autumn, but a day in June. Littlemore was, for those few hours, not so much a retreat as refreshment, a tonic. The church which he had built (and now saw in its completed proportions), with all its personal memories, and containing the graceful memorial to his mother, must have affected him deeply, though he would not dwell upon that. He was contented that all was well and his hope fulfilled.

The Great Western Railway line, with its station at Littlemore, has since been closed, so the journey that could be done in 1868 is no longer possible in this progressive age! It is possible to reach Littlemore by public transport from the centre of Oxford, but not by rail from anywhere.

When the station opened, in 1864, it was quite a humble affair, an oil-lit, wooden building which was destroyed by fire. This was then replaced by a conventional brick-built structure, with waiting-room and the usual offices. The station was erected next to the County Lunatic Asylum (later renamed Mental Hospital), which was provided with its own private siding with access by a small wagon turntable. The weighbridge and weigh-house were built against the Hospital wall. Incidentally, the erection of the Asylum increased the population to 733 in the 1851 census. Littlemore was growing anyway.

The employment situation fluctuated in the wake of the Industrial Revolution and the gradual urbanization of the country districts. In 1819, most of the population had worked as farm labourers. By 1899, this had changed, since most of the farms had been replaced by six market gardens. When plenty of good land was available, market gardening flourished in the area, supplying produce to Oxford greengrocers. That was before the land was lost to house building.

Around this time, Littlemore people also found work in the Oxford Colleges, the John Allen Steam Plough Works, Sandford Brickworks and, of course, the Railway. Later, the Morris motor works at Cowley became the principal employer, and has retained this importance. Taking a long view, Littlemore seems to have been a versatile place, though most of the purely local trades (including the laundry and sawmills) have closed down. A great many premises have changed out of all recognition. The number of public houses has diminished latterly.

Turning back to the railway, and its impact on the village, seems like entering another world. The romantic notion of a sleepy village, isolated from others, gives way to a picture of activity typical of Victorian progress. The station staff, though looking somewhat demure in their photographs, certainly earned their wages by hard work, harder than most would endure today.

There is no doubt that, in addition to passenger traffic, the railway increased the commercial prosperity of Littlemore over the years. An amazing variety of goods was handled, disproportionate to the size of the station:

> Waste paper, alum and china clay, arriving for Messrs Cannon and Clapperton, steel plate for John Allen, the mower and agricultural implement manufacturers, road rollers for repairs, timber both in and out, milk to London twice a day, horses, cattle and sheep, hay and straw, corn, cattle cake and seed. Coal also arrived, together with road-making materials and oil. The station also delivered parcels within a one mile radius...
>
> Richard Lingard

Today it seems almost unbelievable. After nearly a century of passenger service, the last train ran in 1963. Steam railway enthusiasts may find photographs of the single platform station and its staff somewhat nostalgic (even though the yard was at one time infested with rats!). Road transport gradually took the place of trains and the forsaken station became a matter of history - a sad situation which could not have been envisaged in 1868. Whether this line will be re-opened in the future "under new management" is anyone's guess. Even if the working of the old locomotives might nowadays be judged environmentally "unfriendly", one can only regret the passing of the dignified GWR livery.

Littlemore acquired a reputation for being a very healthy place to live and the population continued to increase, although from the Log Book of the Infants' School (kept from 1876 to 1940) it appears that outbreaks of measles and other children's epidemics were fairly common.

On the local government level, progress did not always move very swiftly. At the first meeting of the newly formed Parish Council, in 1894, the provision of street lighting was discussed. This subject was to crop up at regular intervals for some years before the question was finally resolved.

8

The Seasons Pass: Another Century

Newman had firmly believed that he had left Oxford for good on 23 February 1846, though he did finally revisit his beloved University in 1878 with honour, after an absence of just 32 years; but he did not go again to Littlemore. There was not time enough for that possibility. Despite advancing years he remained fully occupied. The village he had loved and served continued on its way, guided by other hands. The city and University of Oxford were expanding.

For many years Father Newman and his constant friend, Dr Bloxam, exchanged letters on or about 22 September, the anniversary of the consecration of Littlemore church, which they never forgot. They were mindful of "all connected with Littlemore, living and dead".

"I called Littlemore my Torres Vedras", wrote Fr Newman, retrospectively (in his *Apologia*). This was a rather obscure allusion to Wellington's campaign in the Peninsular War 1810-11, where the lines of fortification ensured a protracted British victory.

One may wonder what happened to the College after 1846. Some items of information are forthcoming. We know that it did not stay empty or become derelict, even though the collegiate idea was not revived by later occupants. Those who might have developed it in this way never came to settle here to acquire the property, but it never entirely lost the church connection, which ultimately led to its preservation. There are many gaps in the story, when there was nothing to report and life flowed on uneventfully, season by season.

When Newman left Littlemore, his gifted friend from Oriel, the Revd. Charles Marriott, moved in with his printing presses, and with the help of local labour, two or three books were printed there. When Marriott died in 1858, the buildings were left to the Oxford Diocese and were then used as almshouses and a reading room, where newspapers, periodicals, and books were made available for the use of the villagers. Although differing from Newman's original intentions for the College, he would not have disapproved of this charitable service to the people. Perhaps the diocesan authorities were relieved to gain control over what had once seemed a contentious property?

A letter dated 17 May 1886 from the Revd Vernon T Green, vicar of Littlemore from 1872-95, records some of the subsequent history of the College:

> The buildings, which Newman occupied, were purchased by Mr Crawley, and made over to the vicars in perpetuity, as a part of their income. The large room used by Newman as his Library is now applied to the purpose of a Village Reading Room: the chambers where he and his friends lived now form six tenements, three of which I allow to be occupied free of rent by an aged couple and two widows respectively - regardless of what might be said of me by any possible successor in the Incumbency.

More changes of user were yet to happen. In 1915, Canon S. L. Ollard wrote of what Newman had once called "these poor cottages":

> Those houses stand still, turned now into labourers' cottages, but unchanged in structure, and Mr Newman's rooms are still known and pointed out.

> *A Short History of the Oxford Movement*, 1932 edn

The College did not continue permanently in Anglican hands but (following Newman himself) was in due time transferred to Catholic ownership, as will be seen. Before that came an event of some significance in Christian history.

The year 1933 was observed enthusiastically as the Centenary of the Oxford Movement, with mid-July specially highlighted. Naturally, this national celebration had repercussions in Littlemore. Pilgrimage visits were made during that year. On one occasion the singing boys of St. Mary-of-the-Angels Song School performed a setting by Arthur Warrell of Newman's "Lead, kindly Light" in the road outside the College (before its restoration). Those were exciting and joyful times which passed all too quickly. As a follow-up of the centenary an appeal was made for the restoration of St. Mary and St. Nicholas Church and for the building of schools (history repeating itself). Funds were raised in memory of the first donors, whose names were recorded at the rear of the church.

To the outside world the College was still private property, not normally open for inspection, and remained so for twenty years more. 1936 again brought visitors to join with the parishioners of St. Mary and St. Nicholas for another unique occasion, this time celebrating the centenary of their church building.

A modern view of the Church, across Cowley Road.

51

The boys of St. Mary of the Angels singing "Lead Kindly Light" outside Newman's Cottages

9

Later Events: the College

Appropriately, in more recent times, the College was vested in the spiritual descendants of Cardinal Newman, the Fathers of the Birmingham Oratory. This came about in what seems a providential manner. Until 1951 the College (or almshouses) remained the property of the Diocese of Oxford. Then, following a change of vicar, it was decided that as almshouses were no longer needed, it should be put on the market. The asking price was £2,000, a considerable price at that time for such a humble property in poor condition. However, prospects were improving, for it was bought by the Fathers of the Birmingham Oratory who preserved and restored it to resemble its appearance *circa* 1845 as nearly as possible. Newman's modest library was equipped with books, pictures and various mementoes. In the intervening years further restoration work has been done, with pleasing results. The chapel is again used.

In 1987 the College was entrusted to the care of the International Centre of Newman Friends, making it available to all who wish to visit, a place of pilgrimage and study for all Newman friends and scholars, with no taint of commercialism. It is not a place that one "does" as a tourist, en route for the next. One hopes that it may never become that. In charge of the College are Sisters of "The Work", an international Catholic community whose members live in Ambrose Cottage, just behind the College. Fr. Bernard Basset, who knew it well, commented that visitors "now come from all over the world, thoughtful people in their hundreds, drawn by the genius and holiness of the first Vicar of Littlemore, one of the greatest churchmen of all times." Meriol Trevor (1919-2000) lived here while she was writing her lengthy biography of Newman.

To use the word "atmospheric" would be too sensational and could lead to misunderstanding. Although urban noises are not far away, the College and its small rectangular enclosed garden preserve an air of mellow serenity and quiet study. All the stormy controversies have passed. Memories hold no bitterness. The garden, not visible from the road outside, has been planted in an appropriate Old English style. We cannot tell exactly how it looked over 150 years ago, so the present arrangement is the best conjecture. Nothing could seem more English or more peaceful. At first viewing it is a gentle surprise. Newman's garden blooms with such old favourites as lavender and geraniums. We need no reminding that this is the living garden of the man who, in a sermon, had exclaimed: "How much has every herb and flower in it to surprise and overwhelm us." As Canon Francis Bartlett has said, "He must have had a feeling for gardens", remembering also his attachment to the snapdragons growing at Oriel.

It can be said that Newman's words have come true, though not exactly in the sense in which he wrote them:

> "As I made Littlemore a place of retirement for myself, so did I offer it to others."

> *Apologia pro Vita Sua*

Certainly others, including ourselves, are able to enjoy a precious heritage without irritations. A bust of Newman, those rather sharp features mellowed by age, discreetly watches over the garden. The narrow road alongside the College has been aptly named College Lane, which would have been unthinkable in Newman's time here. Certainly, there have been changes.

Now, positioned between the Anglican church and the erstwhile monastery, we find an unmistakably newer building, the Catholic church, dedicated in honour of Newman's visitor in 1845, Blessed Dominic Barberi. Not surprisingly, this was the first church to choose him as its patron. It occupies the site of the old village pound, which was in existence when he came to Littlemore. Dating from 1969, designed by Peter Reynolds, and replacing a previous building of plain rectangular design, this church caused quite a stir at the time of its completion as being aggressively modern. In appearance it can only be described as bizarre and alien to an English village, particularly this one, where we might have expected something more traditional.

> The cluster of glass pyramids projecting above the entrance is a gimmick more suited to a temporary exhibition building and already looks dated... Buff coloured brick, on an irregular five-sided plan.

> Jennifer Sherwood and N. Pevsner, 1974

The glass pyramids seem suggestive of London Bridge Station, as re-designed in 1979. It is possible to get used to the unconventional style, but such asymmetry can be disturbing.

We can imagine what Newman's reaction might be, recalling his words in 1842:

> Misgivings of the mind arise of necessity about the present growing attention which is seen on all sides of us, to Church architecture and Church decoration; not as if all this were not right in itself, but lest we should be too fast about it ...

> Sermon 25

For several consecutive years, a special pilgrimage event in early October brought coachloads of pilgrims from the London, Birmingham and Oxford Oratories to gather here, with a special preacher for the occasion. This pilgrimage commemorates the reception of John Henry

Newman into the Catholic Church, just across the street from where it happened. The celebrations in 1999 included a candlelight procession through the dark streets, from Rose Hill into Littlemore.

On reflection, Littlemore seems a place where Christian rivalries are happily a thing of the past. Its best-known resident is remembered throughout the English-speaking world as the author of a hymn "Lead, Kindly Light" (entitled originally "The Pillar of the Cloud", 1833), "The Dream of Gerontius" (1865) and much else besides. Between those dates came the Littlemore years. With historian's hindsight Father Raleigh Addington wrote:

> Newman's conversion to Rome at Littlemore on that blustery evening in October 1845 was one of the great moments in the religious history of modern times.

It is never likely to be forgotten, though today it would not seem at all dramatic.

Neither his Anglican hymn, "Lead Kindly Light", nor his Catholic ones, "Firmly I Believe" and "Praise to the Holiest", belong particularly to Littlemore. In a wider sense, they are part of the heritage of the whole of Western Christendom.

To complete our exploration of Littlemore in the way of which Belloc and Chesterton would wholeheartedly approve, a pleasant country inn unusually named The Golden Ball is only a few steps away from the Catholic church and opposite the entrance to the College. Newman must have seen it often, though not with the smart appearance that we see today. It was not young then, and had seen countless generations of customers come and go. In 1605, the Golden Ball was a coaching inn.

In the 1920s the only means of lighting was by gas lamps and candles. When the landlords, Morrell's Brewery Ltd., renovated the building, it became the first place in the village to have electricity; rather a paradox for one of the oldest establishments. Despite the inevitable touch of modernisation, the Golden Ball remains true to itself. (Incidentally, Morrells, the oldest surviving family-run business in Oxford, was established in 1782, well before Newman's birth.) The sign now hanging over the doorway is an interesting one, more striking than most, having an unexpected feel of Renaissance art about it. The building has an old world character, as though the years have dealt kindly with it. We might say that the Golden Ball strikes an unashamedly English note. So does the George, even though its roadside setting seems less picturesque now than in the 1840 drawing - and in the meantime the Dragon has become generally unfashionable.

This is still a pleasant village. If it doesn't sound too sentimental, one is closer to the true spirit of England here than in many a stately home and elaborately planned garden. Here is something that has grown organically, not the result of deliberate planning. However real may be the threat of being swallowed up by Oxford, Littlemore's village character endures, like St George's cross.

Not every village is conscious of its history. Here is an exception. The Littlemore Local History Society was formed to promote interest in the preservation of the history of Littlemore and to engage in, support, and co-ordinate, research which has resulted in the collection of quite a large *corpus* of local material.

LITTLEMORE, CIRCA 1840
(Drawing now belonging to Mr. & Mrs. Mattock of Littlemore and Mr. & Mrs. McFie of Oxford)

The George and Dragon Inn, circa 1840

The Altar in Littlemore Church, at which Pusey wept when Newman preached on the Parting of Friends. Note the latter's seven arched re redos, of which he was so proud.

This is more clearly seen in the sketch on p. 27.

58

Envoi

Pilgrimages and research continue; so does the ordinary daily life and work of Littlemore. It cannot live only in the past. In recent years Magdalen College has established an ambitious new "science park" in the locality of Littlemore. The village itself has grown substantially from a hamlet to its present size without losing too much of its rural character; from then until now gathering a remarkable store of memories. Trite as it may seem, however much change may overtake us, such memories from the past remain unchanged and indestructible.

The tidy streets of brick-built houses and their gardens which we see contrast strangely with the rather bleak view depicted when Newman's church was only a few years old. The appearance today is more homely, though much less rural. Spaces have been filled, but were the Tractarian leaders to return, they could still recognise Littlemore. (So perhaps would Mr. Graves.) To help it stay "in good heart and condition" (to use the old phrase) a grant was made in the year 2000 by the Historic Churches Preservation Trust, for essential repairs to St Mary and St Nicholas Church.

How Littlemore will develop as Newman's Cause proceeds towards canonisation is anybody's guess. The present writer makes no predictions. The Cardinal was declared Venerable in 1991. The ongoing process will not be hurried, but Littlemore will still be here (and, one hopes, flourishing), a clean, healthy village.

Bust of Cardinal Newman in the garden at Littlemore. In his own words, "If ever there was a mode of life free from tumult, anxiety, excitement, and fever of the mind, it is the care of a garden"
- Author's photograph.

LITTLEMORE 11

With sorrow marked, and full of years,
As soft eyes harbour unspent tears,
Speaks Littlemore to you and me
Of times gone by and times to be.

Of springtime's smiling incensed day,
When Oxford men walked out that way,
And all was fair in their great cause;
It speaks, too, of the awful pause
When autumn's sere and yellow leaves
Were falling fast and fears were thieves
Of joy and Peace at Littlemore.
A little while, and strife was o'er.

A little while an empty cell
A little while a sad farewell.
And Littlemore's sweet chiming bell
Was sounding Parting's doleful knell.

A century has passed away,
And Littlemore chimes out to-day;
The cradle grey of hopes and fears,
A shrine all-hallowed by the years.

A shrine that evermore shall keep
The memory of saints who weep;
Of friends who wept at Parting sore,
Who wept for grief at Littlemore,
Who now have met around the Throne,
Where parting can no more be known.

As they look down on Littlemore,
Round which their fond affections cling,
What pray they on that holy shore?
That Winter may bring Second Spring?
"Revive thy work in midst of years,
In midst of years, O Lord, make known."
O Littlemore, asperged by tears,
A little more shalt thou be shown.
While Angel faces lost awhile
By him who loved them on us smile.

Desmond Morse-Boycott (1892 – 1979)

Postcript

Anniversaries come and go relentlessly, here as elsewhere. The 200th anniversary of Newman's birth on 21 February 2001 was marked with a special evening service in Littlemore, at which the Bishop of Oxford, the Rt. Revd. Richard Harries, presided. For this occasion, the vicar commissioned the Estonian composer Arvo Pärt to write an anthem for Littlemore, to receive its first performance during the service, in the composer's presence. The words chosen are famous words of Newman which occur at the end of one of his sermons preached at Littlemore (quoted below). Arvo Pärt has called his anthem "Littlemore Tractus". The singers were the choir of St-Martin-in-the-Fields, London, visiting for the occasion.

> May He support us all the day long, till the shades lengthen, and the evening comes, and the busy world is hushed, and the fever of life is over, and our work is done! Then in his mercy may He give us a safe lodging, and a holy rest, and peace at the last.
>
> John Henry Newman, *Wisdom and Innocence*, sermon preached 19 February 1843 in Littlemore.

The author of these words could not have imagined when he delivered them that they might become widely known as an eventide prayer and now be *sung* in his honour here, in the church that he had caused to be built: a good counter-balance to the hymns. The *Tractus* can be regarded not as a minuscule treatise, but as a short and uncontroversial commendation, acceptable to all. No doubt subsequent performances will help spread the knowledge of Newman's words (and their context) and the name of Littlemore still further.

The bicentenary of such a great man's birth could not pass unnoticed. Indeed, the anniversary was also remembered in other places than Littlemore - but that lies outside our present scope.

1801 – 1890

John Henry Cardinal Newman.

Illustrations

Portrait of John Hentry Newman as a young man (frontispiece).
Conjectural ground-plan of Littlemore Priory.
The Seal of Littlemore Priory.
Remains of the Mynchery, as seen in 1845.
Littlemore Church, 1838, engraving by F. B. Delt.
Interior of the Church, looking eastward, as it was in Newman's time: from a sepia sketch of 1839.
Caricature sketch, 1844, showing the school, Church, and "Mr Newman's building".
Newman's buildings, intended to form the nucleus of a monastic house.
Another view of the church, with extracts from the Baptismal Register.
Drawing of the church by Mr. Walsh, a former inhabitant of Littlemore.
The Church of Blessed Dominic Barberi, Littlemore.
Littlemore Railway Station, two views.
A modern view of the Church across the Cowley Road.
Singing "Lead, kindly Light" outside the College, 1933
The George and Dragon, *circa* 1840.
The Altar in Littlemore Church
Newman's garden. (Photograph by the author.)
Medallion portrait of John Henry, Cardinal Newman.

Notes

1. The older spelling seems to have been Littlemoor, although some of the early spellings in documents do not confirm this, e.g. Luthlemoria (c. 1130), Litlemora (c. 1191), Lutlemore (1220).

2. For details of the Sandford Preceptory, see the present author's *Traces of the Templars.*

3. To quote Dr Anthony R. Wagner, Richmond Herald: "The use of seals by corporate bodies to authenticate documents was a practical necessity, but it was by no means necessary that the devices on the seals should be armorial. Many of them displayed the figures of patron saints or non-heraldic combinations of emblems."

4. Mr Graves's information is slightly inaccurate. Dr Pusey did not exercise any *official* ministry in Littlemore.

5. While it is true that the dedication combined that of the University Church and the local Priory (the Mynchery), it is questionable whether the bishop or any of the clergy concerned would have wanted to commemorate the disgraced convent - or even if they knew much about it.

6. It has been tentatively suggested that Pugin may have had a hand in the Church's design.

7. Today Oxfordshire as a whole is not a heavily forested county. It has been estimated (*circa* 1992) that only about 5% of the land is woodland, contrasted with over 60% arable land.

8. Possibly a spiteful confusion with the Mynchery.

9. It is of interest that long before Beethoven became popular in England as a composer, his music was played (privately) in Littlemore.

10. They had lived at Rose Hill, near Littlemore.

11. The poem on Littlemore must have been written in the mid-1930s. It was published in a school magazine in 1936. The poet was a great lover of Littlemore and a considerable authority on the Oxford Movement, from the Anglican standpoint.

Bibliography

Victoria County History - Oxfordshire vols. IV and V

Jennifer Sherwood and Nickolaus Pevsner	*The Buildings of England - Oxfordshire* Penguin Books, 1974
J.H. Newman	*Apologia pro Vita Sua* Oxford University Press
J.H. Newman	*A Packet of Letters*, a Selection from the Correspondence Ed. Joyce Sugg Clarendon Press, Oxford, 1983
R.D. Middleton	*Newman and Bloxam* Oxford University Press, 1947
S.L. Ollard	*A Short History of the Oxford Movement* A.R. Mowbray & Co., 1932
Richard Lingard	*Princes Risborough-Thame-Oxford Railway* Oxford Publishing Co., 1978
Bernard Basset, S.J	*Newman at Littlemore* Friends of Newman, n.d.
J. Arnatt et al.	*The Changing Faces of Littlemore and Sandford* Robert Boyd Publications 1996 (O.P.)
Dennis W. Coombs	*A History of Littlemore* Unpublished typescript, 1975
Meriol Trevor	1. *The Pillar of the Cloud* 2. *Light in Winter* Macmillan and Co. 1962

Index

Acknowledgements

Thanks are due to the Revd Bernhard Schünemann, Vicar of St Mary and St. Nicholas, Littlemore, for his help and encouragement.

Grateful thanks also to Mrs J. Arnatt and the Littlemore Local History Society for much information from their archives, to the Bodleian Library, Oxford, to various friends who have shown a kindly interest, not least to Debbie Nunn and Maisie Robson for their work on the manuscript and typesetting.

Publisher's Note